Photo by Thom Jackson

Rob Steventon has been peddling poetry since 2013 and has been Champion of Manchester's Word War and York's Say Owt poetry slams. He is the founder and director of Punk in Drublic Poetry, a regular event at which performance poetry and stand-up comedy violently clash. All of Punk in Drublic Poetry's door fees are donated to Mustard Tree Homelessness charity.

Rob is not a millionaire. He would be grateful if you could lend him a tenner.

"Rob Steventon made his millions through acerbic, authentic, down-and-dirty verse. Not millions of quid, but millions of jabs, swipes, tears, laughs, hugs and puns. He targets landlords, human resources and quacks, and embraces love, friends, Manchester and his mum. And, call me a traditionalist, but his poems have meter and rhyme like poetry is meant to. Discuss. To sum up, in the univocalism deployed so well by the poet himself: Rob's book: dog's bollocks."
Janine Booth, poet, writer & activist

"His words are inventive, surprising, political, accessible, relatable and really laugh-out-loud funny."
Dominic Berry, Glastonbury Festival poet-in-residence

"As it's in my nature to take the piss, it's difficult writing a quote for Rob as there is simply no angle you can mock him from. Despite his dashing stage presence, effortless style, enviable talents and infuriating work ethic he is still widely regarded as one of the nicest guys in the game, and rightly so. It's no coincidence that performance poetry became more popular once Rob got involved."
Thick Richard, spoken word artist

*To the wonderful people
of Manchester.*

HOW I MADE
MY MI££IONS
Rob Steventon

Flapjack Press
flapjackpress.co.uk

Exploring the synergy between performance and the page

Published in 2021 by Flapjack Press
Salford, Gtr Manchester
⊕flapjackpress.co.uk
f Flapjack Press ✔FlapjackPress ▶ Flapjack Press

ISBN 978-1-8381185-7-0

Illustrations & cover by Sonny Ross
⊕sonnyross.com ✔sonnyross

Author photo by Thom Jackson
⊕deadbasicstudios.com

Printed by Imprint Digital
Exeter, Devon
⊕digital.imprint.co.uk

FSC

MAN CHE STER
A UNESCO City
of Literature

Contents

How I Made My Millions

I : I'm not a poet

To those who have bought this book seeking insight on the accumulation of wealth, I apologise for having sucked you in with such a misleading title.

If it is money making tips that you seek in the literature from independent poetry publishers, it's likely that you've not done your research and it's likely that you won't fit within what would be considered my target demographic.

I'd like to thank you nonetheless, as you've unwittingly helped – in a very small way – towards the title of this poetry collection becoming something more rooted in reality.

I feel immeasurably humbled to have the opportunity to publish a poetry collection, so I oughtn't waste too much time taking the piss out of any potential people who are unwittingly helping me towards making another.

I also feel immeasurably humbled to be able to call myself a poet; I feel rich in nourishing friendship, support and solidarity from the poetry community in the north of England. These wonderful people have not only helped me develop my repertoire as a performer and a writer, but blessed me with invaluable insights, made often pants-pissingly funny memories with me and become reliable and valuable friends.

Ultimately, these people, their collective arsenal of anecdotes, their life-affirming insights and the parties, poetry gigs and professional opportunities they've shared with me make up for more fulfilment than any level of material wealth ever could.

They and their insights are my millions.

Wealth and financial gain will never cease to be some form of incentive in the making of art. However, wealth has become such an elusive mirage of a concept in these increasingly brutal and unequal times that its direct influence in quantifying the value of art seems redundant.

It would be of the most pious and disingenuous idiocy for me to pretend that I don't aspire to material wealth and thus get excited by the prospect of being able to make money by doing what I love – making poetry. However, what I seek to express in this book is that the gratitude I have for the people around me and who have guided me through my journey as a poet, makes me feel rich. As Kurt Vonnegut so pertinently put it, *"To practice any art, no matter how well or badly, is a way to make your soul grow. So do it.".*

Poetry has by no means always been my art. It might be a custom to precede a poetry collection with an autobiographical forward about how it became my art.

Well, the poems that make up this first chapter are poems that are more of perception than reflection – more about how I see the world I live in than about me. So, the story of how I became a poet will have to come a bit later.

I have things to get off my chest first.

We live in a society where rents are skyrocketing while wages are flatlining.

We live in a society where billions of pounds of public money are channelled into the cronies of government ministers, whilst being sucked out of the welfare budget and forcing the closure of things like Sure Start Centres.

We live in a society where the streets, alleyways and door-ways of our cities have become the makeshift bedrooms for a burgeoning number of unfortunate people, whilst the richest 1% are accumulating more wealth than ever before.

All of these things, frankly, boil my piss.

They make me so irrefutably angry.

I feel that these things are utterly tragic.

There isn't necessarily any righteousness or virtue in me writing a chapter of poems about how angry these things make me, but when tapped into at the right angle, anger is a fountain of comedic value.

I've been performing stand-up comedy for nearly as long as I've been performing poetry and one of the insights that I've been blessed with from that is the comedic value in anger.

I feel that comedic value is something that has to have a presence on the criteria for what makes good art. I feel that tragedy and the inevitable anger that it prompts is an essential part of comedy.

I hope that in these first poems you can find that value and enjoy the soothing quality of irony and comedy that has helped me through the most difficult times in life.

As Jack Dee noted, *"Comedy and tragedy are two sides of the same coin. A talent in one area might also lead to a predisposition in the other."*.

Walking Lawsuit

I'm not a poet,
I'm a walking lawsuit.
Rip off other's style,
bestow it like a fly in your soup.

Deploy brute force of forgery
and hope it takes root.
When I've finished this piece
I'll be inundated with disputes.

This whole piece is plagiarised
from those with more creative prowess.
When it comes to poetic devices,
I'm endowed less.

I'll drown out my shortcomings
with boisterousness and loudness.
And vulgar sexual imagery;
tonight, I'll be the foulest.

(Thick Richard does a better one of these,
it's called 'Scum of the Earth'.) [1]
This poem's shaft's null of the length
and it's also null of the girth.

I don't know why I bothered
or why to it I gave birth.
I take the sexy from dyslexia,
the lurid I unearth.

I'm not a poet,
I'm a clueless quizmaster.
Every Monday night I bamboozle
and curate a disaster.

Pumping trivia to punters
on a school night, getting plastered.
But having questions that make sense
isn't something that I've mastered...

"*Romanian city Bucharest is the capital of which nation?*"
"*Name the breed and quantity of dogs in the film* 101 Dalmatians."

I'm not a poet,
I'm a man with mental illness
who just writes about it.
My father, he abandoned me
(and I still cry at night about it).

My foot constantly in my mouth
and I'm constantly contrite about it.
Shouting shit's my raison d'être, see,
it's just me and my plight without it.

Let's not hide behind verbosity,
not all that is gold is glittering.
No one really wants to hear
a lanky wanker being self-pitying.

My mind's chock-a-block
like Ashton Road after a City game.
Only frauds present life's beauty
whilst obscuring the gritty things.

People tried to talk me down from this,
worrying that the exposure may
go to my head and bring on
aspirations that are throwaway.

I'll stand and shout shit on this stage
until I'm told to go away.
The only shoulder I can cry on's
the hard shoulder on the motorway.

...and I don't even drive.
I failed my test when I was seventeen.

Maybe not every tool's blunt
that occupies my task box, but
I'm so full of shit, give me an enema,
I'd fit in a matchbox. [2]

---

[1] Thick Richard's poem 'Scum of the Earth' is in the collection *Vaudavillain* (*sic*) [Flapjack Press, 2017].
[2] These final lines reference critic Christopher Hitchens's comments on the then recently deceased Reverend Jerry Falwell Sr.

The Desperate Jobseeker's Blues

Applying, applying, applying, applying,
applying, applying, applying, applying...

Applying, applying, applying, applying –
it's all coming back with shit.

There are few tasks that are quite less gratifying
than hours every night to commit
authoring paragraphs, whoring my attributes.
Missed the mark again, got the desperate jobseeker's blues.

Five years ago, pulling pints naively stocked
with a Bachelor's Degree in the Arts;
not expecting the world to fall at my feet,
just not wanting to fall on my arse.

See, I've got three jobs now but they're all zero hours.
They've cut off the leccy, I'm having cold showers.
Should be more astute with the options I choose,
haemorrhaging cash with the desperate jobseeker's blues.

These HR departments with their buzzwords and jargon
are becoming my enemies;
I'm a qualified grafter with goals to chase after,
but embellish my qualities.

Their poorly spelled adverts fail GCSEs,
an apostrophe in the word 'vacancies',
they're the kind who leave shit TripAdvisor reviews –
fuck you human resources, the desperate jobseeker's blues.

"Competitive rates of pay!"
it proclaims, before revealing £7.50.
I repeat: *there's no apostrophe in the word 'vacancies'*
between the letters 's' and 'e'!

…not in any context.
Or an 'a' in the fucking word 'competitive'.
Call up my mother to tell her the news;
rejected again, got the desperate jobseeker blues.

The train to work's not a want it's a need,
walk twenty miles there my feet start to bleed.
Tempted to start flogging shit eighths of weed
and with the profits start bribing, indeed.
Checking my junk mail folder for hidden news,
banana skin on my career path, I've got the jobseeker blues.

Will my girlfriend forgive me if sexual favours
are part of the bargain for fruits of my labour?
'Cause I'll suck and I'll fuck, I'll be fucked and I'll rim,
if you'll just make my job prospects a bit less grim!

Hanging my tea bags to dry and re-use,
it's gaffer tape holding together my shoes
as I sanitise my political views
under the spell of the desperate jobseeker's blues.

I turned up to my interview stinking of booze
'cause I've given up now; got the desperate jobseeker's blues.

Cashback

A univocalism in 'A'.

Cashback?
Cashback?!
"Pah!"
Bank wants that back man!

Catch cash, pay back what can.
Always lay a savvy plan.

Back at drab shanty pad,
ants attack man's snack stash bad.

Chap snacks at saggy salad.
Chap casts wants, sways at sad ballad.

Chap gasps at hard facts à la bank.
Wayward chap lays back, blank.

Chap asks pal, "Cash? ... *Pffffft*, thanks."
Chap's arm fat, as chap has had many sad wanks.

Chap's snazzy pals chat bland Manc drawl.
Twats bark black cab catcalls.

Wavy chap slams back flat – drab hallway falls.
Can't stand sharp pangs – clasps achy balls. [3]

Chap's fantasy walks past; sassy lass – Natash.
Happy 'Tash snarls sarcasm at chap.

Taps away black fag ash.
Chap walks away, abash...

Chap's gaffa grants chap a grand! Yay!
Plays jazzy tracks all day…

bags Havana vacay!
Chap swans away drag garms – sashay away.

Chap's jaw clamps – MDMA.
Adamantly, chap starts day.

"Bank all cash! Stash!" chap says.
"Bank all cash! Stash!"

---

[3] The word 'achy' appears in the Oxford, Cambridge and Collins English Dictionaries with the spellings 'achy' and 'achey'. [4]

[4] In Billy Ray Cyrus's 1992 hit single, 'Achy Breaky Heart', the former spelling was used. [5]

[5] If Billy Ray can make millions of dollars using such spelling, I can bloody well do so in my poem.

We were simple Billy Goats, content on our side of the valley
with no need to challenge our perspective.
With trouble out of sight and mind, kind spirits we could rally,
grazing in good company as a collective.

Across the bridge, up to the hillside to make ourselves fat,
we'd heard that pastures greener did await.
Good tidings tweeted through the air in warm and friendly chat.
We were nourished to listen and validate.

We'd bear our souls in 280 characters in good faith
and receive tweets from others empathically.
We'd heard of a troll beneath the bridge, but remained unscathed.
Too long don't read, don't doubt the hill's sanctity.

Our side of the valley started fading from its brighter green,
so we travelled one by one across the bridge.
One of the Billy Goats said, "Greener pastures I have seen,
we'll ascend and all will see my courage."

Treading with care, across the bridge, yearning for peaceful scrolling.
The first from our bubble they were confronted.
Their simple innocence it was corrupted by cruel trolling.
Their tools for understanding truth were blunted.

The rest of us heard calls from down the valley but doubted them.
One of us said that it was their own fault.
Fake news stories from the valley, they said –
    ban those who transmit them.
To the wounds obtained from comment boxes, apply salt.

Another crossed the bridge and heard a compelling theory
of how the need for pastures green was just a hoax.
Others of us, of comment-box-combat had grown weary.
Fear was left when context was sucked out from jokes.

And jokes were part of our diet, jokes helped grow understanding
of our difference and to appreciate it.
Jokes provided to life's descents a soft and cushioned landing,
applying joy to tragedies belated.

But we descended and berated…

"That's not a person in the comments box, that's not even a person!"
"Find his Mum's profile and tell her she should be ashamed of her son."
"Don't listen to apologies, his sincerity is swerving."
"Look, a dumpster fire, let's throw more petrol on and watch it worsen."

"AIBU, is it undue to doubt this weak appeaser?"
"Don't like my enemies, but not my enemies' enemies either."
The troll sowed seeds of doubt and from that good faith it did lever.
Comment-box-combat took hold over all like a cold fever.

The mute button, the block button, the ban button grew weak.
Our abbreviations had sucked out all meaning,
complicating defending the different and the meek.
All good tidings tweeting converted to screaming.

Rhetoric turned violent; the troll was confronted with sharp spears.
The only solution is that he's slain.
But then someone intervened, to listen and provide an ear
and began to learn the troll was also in pain.

But no! We must inflict our wrath, some argued with fervency.
We must maim and inflict pain upon the troll.

No time for a fair trial, we must act quick with urgency.
We should display his mangled corpse upon the knoll.

There's virtuous and villainous and the troll is the latter.
Redemption is simply out of the question.
We must chop off his limbs and all must witness his blood splatter.
All must understand the outcome of transgressions.

The troll had lived a hard life and knew of only combat.
It was the only way the troll got validation.
The troll shamed others, as for years with only shame he'd sat.
He knew not of compassion or consideration.

Shame and suspicion were the troll's truths, colouring his perspective.
Stunting his lucid brain like a lobotomy.
Truth's not simply one view point, truth is plain – it is objective.
But truth can't always be boiled down to a dichotomy.

In the absence of compassion, combat does seem entertaining
and everyday communication can turn snide.
But in this story, whether toxic influences started waning,
was on us Billy Goats and the troll to decide.

Doctors.
Doctors?
Pffffff.
Who do they think they are?
Magic Medicine Men?

Oh, I'm so smart, I progressed
and attained far enough
in education that I got accepted
into Medical School, studied
and worked thoroughly for six years
and then started a job
where I usually work eighty hours a week
and have to see people die.
And I have the temerity to tell people
what to do to best support their health.

Don't. Think. So.

Just because you see people
in every conceivable state of health
and decide on a treatment
bespoke to their needs
doesn't mean you get to hold a viewpoint
on it that's considered valid.

Especially not on *my* health.

I once
knew a person who died.
The Doctors didn't make them survive.

I read on an internet forum
about a Doctor who thought
that all the other Doctors had gotten it wrong.
Now that's a Doctor I can get behind.

Dr Fauci, Dr Whitty, Dr Davies, Dr Who,
Dr Feelgood, Dr Oetker, Dr Cooper Clarke, Dr Pepper,

with such a variety of views to choose from,
how can we decide which ones take seriously?

If it was such a noble profession,
then not one of them
would have ever gotten anything wrong
at all in their own career

...and I'm supposed to believe
that they're mostly decent people
who work incredibly hard
and amongst the most altruistic of us?

Yeah right!

City v Grimsby

A univocalism in 'I'.

Jim McKinny, thirty-six, driving his BMW riskily,
slyly skids his whip in slip with simplicity.
"Winning!" Jim glibly spits,
lighting his cig with skill whilst shifting it in fifth.

City v Grimsby, by six.
Timing it tightly.
Swift! Swift Mr McKinny!
Jim's wishing City finish winny.

Jim sits by pitch, "KICK IT!"
City striking with might, "KICK HIM!"
City whipping Grimsby's tits,
Grimsby still sitting in nil.
"Shit."

City win six nil, Jim grips his pint, wildly sings.
Jim is windmilling his limbs,
licking his slips, sniffing his ching.
Childishly picking fights in wings.

Whilst giving Grimsby jip,
spirits slip.
Pints spill, piss drips.
Jim splits his lip.

Jim's Mrs rings,
lividly chiding Jim.
Rigidly pissy with Jim's tipsy trips.

Jim's Mrs is sick by his tipsy slips.
"WHY JIM, WHY?
DIGNITY JIM, IT'S DIGNITY!"
Jim sits in sinbin

"Thing is, right—"
"ZIP IT, JIM! ZIP IT!"
Jim's Mrs spits.

Jim is living in this grim prism – Blighty.

Jim's Blighty is:
fish 'n' chips,
insipid Right Wing thinking,
pints 'n' tits.

"You Can Use Poetry to Sell Anything These Days..."

A handful of failed sales pitch limericks.
(Please get in touch if you think I could help sell your product or
services – I charge reasonable and competitive rates.)

---

i.

When Facetime and phone calls don't have depth
And under-stimulate you to death,
Let your senses be thrown
With the new Smell-O-Phone!
You can chat whilst checking friends' breath.

---

ii.

Your dating apps leave no match in sight?
You're feeling your prospects aren't bright?
A picture tip that's sound:
Upload it upside down.
It makes people accidentally swipe right.

(Don't actually do this – it's a dick move.)

iii.

Balancing Covid safety and dating
Makes getting intimate seem frustrating.
Go to the shop and ask
For our Kissing Hole Mask.

(On full safety approval, we're waiting.)

iv.

Don't dare put in effort that's lacklustre
Or taint our class's tranquillity with fluster.
If you can't just calmly breathe
Then please fuck off and leave.
I'm the Angry Meditation Instructor.

v.

An investment opportunity
Generously tipped to you by me;
A plan rooted in rigours,
Please invest six figures
In my career of poetry!

Morgz

A univocalism in 'O'.

Sprogs' toons stop, Morgz clocks on, gold forks pop yolks.
Now on *Good Morn'*[6], Morgz 'n' BoJo concoct bollocks
on poor brown folk.

"Don't worry!" crows Morgz. "No dross ont' TV box!"
Morgz; jobsworth shocky-jock
oddly croons on to gormy flock.
Slyly shoots slop from floppy cock.

Johnson's floppy gold top rolls down front of fod.
"Oh, hoho, jolly good," boys plot.
Good folks' folly, bro to Tory clots.
Cohort of Corbyn? Golly gosh, no room for Trots!

"Jolly good, Mr Mogg!" Morgz hosts grotty monopoly,
Morgz clots old folks' colostomy,
Morgz's fod proports monotony,
Morgz won't stop short of TV lobotomy.

Tomorrow on *Good Morn'*, strong look from Tommy Robz.
Morgz blows bloody scorn on yobs.
Swoon on Don?
Look, Morgz knows how to do good sloppy blowjobs.

No synonym works for Morgz.
Why won't Morgz sod off?

---

[6] Morgz has of course now left *Good Morning Britain*, but that in no way changes
the sentiment of this poem and happily extends to anything else he'll crop up on.

Travel's a necessity, but leaves me feeling frail.
I wouldn't mind a seat or space to stand and sip an ale,
space in the vestibule consumed by commuter's travail,
crushed against a door engulfed in stenches, noxious, stale.
These departure times are about as much use as flattened Braille,
my patience has shrunk to the size of an egg of a quail,
a migraine's been induced from the all-toil that it entails;
to get to work on time, it's a far-fetched fairytale.
I've bloody lost two hours' wages from the delay, I'll
spend 'til 10 a.m. hiding my hate through a thin veil.
The taxpayer pays three times more since British Rail's sale;
compared with ours, other countries' ticket costs pale.
I'd have been quicker holding an umbrella up against a gale.
As I alight, I'm met with queues just faster than a snail.
Met by some G4S bully boy who looks hard as nails
with a bodycam and a beer gut the size of a sperm whale;
he murders fare evaders and he's just been released on bail.
I'm coughing phlegm up thanks to plumes of exhaust I've inhaled.
It's as good for the environment as drilling for shale.
Serco's profits soar while my punctuality fails.
Uber's stocks boom – there's fights for a taxi to hail.
I hope you step on an upturned plug, Northern Rail.
What has been found is inefficiency's Holy Grail.
Scrap your 1970's trains and throw your directors in jail.

The Desperate House Hunter's Blues

Scouring listings and listings and listings and listings and
listings and listings and listings...

Scouring listing on Zoopla and Rightmove and SpareRoom
and ads in the *Evening News*.

As my tenancy ticks like a time bomb,
I worry it will reach the end of its fuse.
On a shoebox with back-alley brothel views,
my credit check failed; got the desperate house hunter's blues.

It's not fine to smoke or have pets or have debts,
but it's fine to profit out of squalor.
My income has taken a downturn this year,
but my landlord wants more of my dollar.

He tells me to tighten my belt and my collar,
says he knows bailiffs personally he can holler.
He's a football thug Tory with tribal tattoos
and I'm lining his pension; the desperate house hunter's blues.

I turn up to a derelict shell in Ardwick
that is host to a studio flat.
When I ask where the fridge in the kitchen is,
Amber, the letting agent starts to laugh.

"Who needs a fridge these days with Uber Eats and that?"
Perhaps those who want to store fresh food intact.
"And these restaurants all have five-star reviews."
They're out of my price range; desperate house hunter's blues.

"If you're after compact, you can't get much compacter.
Walls meet at acute angles – check with your protractor.
Heating stuck on high like a nuclear reactor.
These pea soup green bath tiles have such a wow factor.

Just send us two months' wages, if it's this place you choose."
I'll just live off Space Raiders; the desperate house hunter's blues.

There've been times where my cash hasn't stretched the whole
    month
and eviction's come close like a vicious affront.
I'd be fucked if it weren't for friends, I'll be blunt.
The top cause of homelessness is tight landlord cunts.

We should all go on strike and just simply refuse
to keep lining their pockets; the desperate house hunter's blues.

In 2005, £70 a week for half an hour's work a day, five days a week was, for a fifteen-year-old, a fucking lucrative deal. Such a wage would likely stand out to the fifteen-year-old of 2021 as a fucking lucrative deal as well.

Here's how Our Guy earned it.

A lovely old lady in Our Guy's home town had lost the necessary agility and strength to tend to the dozen-or-so Australian Terriers that she bred for the Crufts championships. She required an agile young assistant to come into the kennels built in the garden of her house and clean up every last drop of shit from these poor mutts, before feeding them a meal of microwave defrosted tripe.

Twice a day.

Five days a week.

The smell of the dog shit paled in comparison to the oppressive, repugnant stench that wafted into Our Guy's lungs as he opened the microwave door each weekday morning and afternoon. It made him nauseous, but his nausea didn't begin to chip away at how lucrative an employment opportunity he had found.

This employment opportunity was one that he had gladly held as a teenager for about eighteen months. On his bike ride to and from school, he fed, watered and cleaned the shit from the kennels of those Australian Terriers five days a week. The old lady treated Our Guy relatively well, greeting his regular tardiness with patience and consideration.

The experience was invaluable to Our Guy for a number of reasons – the most important of which being that whenever his work ethic is called into doubt, he now can sanctimoniously and self-righteously proclaim that he shovelled shit for a living to get to where he is now.

In reality, it was a well-remunerated bit of side-graft he had as a hapless and lazy teenager, which ultimately embedded unrealistic expectations of what constitutes a reasonable disposable income.

II : On this whole entire planet,
there's nowhere else I'd rather be

In September 2009, I was dropped off by a very city traffic-flustered Mum outside a tower block on Salford Precinct, to move into student accommodation and commence a Batchelor's Degree in Music at The University of Salford.

From the 5th floor view, I inspected the post-war council estates of Salford that paved the path to Manchester city centre and what would become my new home town.

I am a drummer and I was filled with a weird concoction of excitement and trepidation at the prospect of pursuing a career as a musician. Twelve years on, my zig-zagged career path as a performer has taken a completely different turn – and I couldn't possibly be more pleased that it has.

So, how did it happen?

Aside from having the obligatory adolescent poetic discoveries ('The Melancholy of Ted Hughes', 'The Profanity of John Cooper Clarke' and 'The Wit of Scroobius Pip'), I had no real interest in performance poetry until one day in May 2010.

I was working at a bar called The Thirsty Scholar on Oxford Road in Manchester around my studies. At a gig hosted there, a spectacled Mancunian gobshite commandeered the mic and transfixed the attention of the entire pub on his diatribe of sardonic satire and profanity-laden performance poetry. His name was Thick Richard and his performance blew-me-the-fuck-away.

It turned out Thick Richard was the cousin of a previous band mate I'd had and I started to attend gigs at which Thick Richard was performing as often as I could.

My friend Ollie Winnington took me to see Kae Tempest's *Brand New Ancients* show in 2013 and my friend Chris Godber introduced me to the work of American poet Buddy Wakefield. I learned that spoken word poetry was an art in – and of – itself.

It was a few years of penning regrettable pieces that certainly won't feature in this book before I plucked up the courage to make the transition on stage; from behind the drum kit to centre stage with a microphone.

Shortly after graduating University, I got a job at my favourite pub in Manchester, The Marble Arch. Fitting gigs with bands around long working weeks in a bar was very tiring, but equipped me with the necessary work ethic and resilience to pursue a career in the creative industries. But in 2014, I was admitted to the Manchester Royal Infirmary in a haze of dizziness and was subsequently diagnosed with Type 1 diabetes.

Having worked in bars for years served me well in having to then deal with pricks on a daily basis.

Dr Pepper, what's the worst that can happen?

Hyperglycaemia, in my case.

I remember the stay in hospital being something that flooded me with gratitude for all that the city of Manchester had given me, in its frequent hilarity, regular toil and occasional joy.

I wanted to express this.

Unaware that there was an established scene for spoken word nights in Manchester, I started to perform poems at music open mic nights. People invariably would balk at the compere of these nights proclaiming *"Next up, we've got a poet!"*.

The experience of performing to a disinterested crowd was utterly invaluable and gave me the confidence to suggest to The Marble Arch that we start to run an open mic night there *just* for poetry. I learned quickly that if I was writing material to be performed, it should be as engaging and accessible to a non-poetry audience as possible and avoid the tropes of a traditional 'recital'. As someone with dyslexia and dyspraxia, I have cognitive impairments that affect tasks like reading text aloud, so committing my pieces to memory and focusing on a performance that utilised the space and engaged interactively with the audience meant that I was playing to my strengths.

In 2015, I was employed as a Stage Manager at Manchester's Comedy Store. My role entailed making show reports on each performer's set and the audience's response. Spending so much time observing comperes orchestrating compliance, concurrence and laughter with such dynamism inspired me. Even after having racked up enough hours in my role to recognise formulas, set-lines and riffing techniques used, I was still in awe of the improvised art of compering and improvisational stand-up comedy.

I soon gave it a go, to much better avail than I expected.

With the aim of converging the worlds of poetry and comedy and creating a space in which a broader range of performative styles could be explored, I established Punk in Drublic Poetry in March 2017.

My job as host and compere at Punk in Drublic entails performing poetry and comedy and maintaining a level of jocular interaction with the audience. Having a regular audience returning to the night has necessitated me writing at a much quicker rate and being prepared to test ideas on stage.

Punk in Drublic has grown hugely since its conception and now runs stages at both the Bluedot and Kendal Calling festivals. In 2020, it won the Saboteur Award for 'Best Regular Spoken Word Night in the UK'.

Having seen homelessness skyrocket in my home city since the ushering in of the coalition Conservative government in 2010, I wanted to be able to do something to support services working with homeless people. I decided that Punk in Drublic should donate all of its door fees to Mustard Tree Homelessness charity and it has, since its conception, raised more than £10,000 for them.

Punk in Drublic has become my home as a performer and the setting for the testing of many of the ideas that made it to this book. Whilst I run the night independently, I wouldn't be able to do so without the support, solidarity and practical help of the poets, comedians, promoters and venue managers of Manchester who have allowed me to endeavour such an idea. Elena at Reasons to be Cheerful in Burnage, Deano at The Old Pint Pot in Salford and Andi at Lock91 have all hosted my flapping around worrying about something relating to the running of a gig. Thick Richard, Dominic Berry, Dave Viney and more have provided me with much needed feedback after performances I've done at gigs that I've organised.

Performance, comradeship, solidarity, hilarity, joy.

I am blessed to live in a city that has allowed me to pursue these things that I yearn for.

The next poems in this book are dedicated to that city and the wonderful people and places it is host to.

Manchester.

A student card, some keys, a paltry pocket of bank notes.
A small interest free overdraft to help keep me afloat.
A persistent anxious quiver and lump in my throat.
An arsenal of social skills made up of flatter and gloat.

A sprawling Salford campus and the neglect it surrounds.
A view across this fair city, a bloom of greys and browns.
A view of architectural glories that have since been stricken down.
The view that I'm sure inspired 'Evidently Chickentown'.

Nineteen-year-old naiveties, to which I held with piety.
Like how chemical stimulants would quell social anxiety.
How adding Slayer to the party playlist made for welcome variety.
How my work and health and studies need neither rest nor sobriety.

Naiveties I knew were naiveties, but held, asinine.
Of hard to swallow truths, the future would be a goldmine.
Looking back on the beliefs that back then seemed fair and benign.
Beliefs held in good faith by me, back in 2009.

*"£3000 a year in just tuition fees is hardly fair and there's no chance
whatsoever that anyone could ever consider increasing them further."*

*"Now we've got Rage Against the Machine to Christmas number one,
instigating real social change will be a doddle!"*

"Now that Nick Griffin's been humiliated on Question Time, *there's
no chance anyone will ever take anyone from the far right seriously."*

*"When I'm thirty, looking back at these times from the living room of
the house that I own, I'll thank myself for laying the groundwork for
such an illustrious and fruitful career."*

I remember walking back to my student halls from a party.
Having run myself over with my words like Brian Harvey.
Feeling hopeless and inadequate and bitter like Campari.
If I'd known what the next years would hold,
would I have judged myself so harshly?

All aboard, all aboard, all drink-addled limbs
swing like blunted swords.

All entranced by the screens on their phones,
all haemorrhaging their student loans.

Playing David Guetta through the tinny speakers,
egging on exhibitionists and attention seekers.

This girl's missing her ex-boyfriend and this guy's missing a shoe.
Destination is frayed nerve ends on the Number 42.

I've just finished my night shift and I'm bostin' for a piss.
I killed someone in a past life and my punishment is this.

Some space cadet offers me a balloon of nitrous oxide gas.
I gasp convulsively hoping that it'll make the minutes pass.

Someone extinguishes their cigarette on a randomer's suede jacket.
And that incoherent football thug persists with his racket:

> "U-N-I … T-E-D,
> UNITED ARE TEAM FOR ME,
> WITH A KNICK KNACK PADDY WHACK
> GIVE A DOG A BONE—"

Fuck this, I'm getting off
and walking home.

Ode to Abdul's

4 a.m. orders, marauding for starch in polystyrene boxes
with grease in the corners and conspicuous stains.

My stomach, the poor thing, recoiling in shame
from the sordid, ravenous banquet that caused this –
for four quid I bought this pain.

Zero-star food hygiene ratings,
to sober eyes it's nauseating,
their TripAdvisor page is scathing
and now deep in regret I'm bathing.

Coagulated yellow, glowing loosely
off my pillow from the pungent garlic mayo
that's necessitated frantic scrubbing
and chemical fumigating.

What the fuck did I order?!

Chips and cheese with a side of Legionnaires' disease,
slathered with ease in toxic, viscous grease,
all for what's left in my pocket, please…

I declared chemical warfare on my physiology.
Now, with my body, I must make peace.

The Marble Arch

For all of the scores settled,
for our appearances dishevelled,
in four walls that saw the suffragettes
and two world wars, we're nestled.

It beacons ever stronger as days
leave us feeling bitter.
Its glow of solidarity
to our dark days, an emitter.

We clock off and on amber relief,
our wages we can fritter.
We adjourn all that divides us
and fighting people over Twitter.

I arrived alone; eyes glued to phone,
reluctant to switch off.
Mosaic tiles on my eyes,
Mosaic Hops on my nose, I quaff.

Chirpy syntax awakens my awareness,
eyes rise up aloft.
A range of backgrounds and characters
from the binman to the toff.

A girl descends down sloping floor to bar,
the terrain it confounds.
A longing look through lacking funds,
she slowly counts her pounds.

"I've too much month
at the end of my money," she frowns.
A stranger intervenes and says,
"Put this one on my round."

Here's a Punk in Drublic poet
purporting pissed-up propaganda
whilst poor, perplexed punters
to his poppycock must pander.

Poorly punctuated prose pours,
people peer through for a gander.
Whether at him or with him,
the laughter quells all grief and anger.

As Rees-Mogg lounges arrogantly
on Westminster's green upholstery,
on our green upholstered benches
we bring plenty to the paltry.

Booze drowns out our fears
and we indulge in a cold treat.
Boos drowned out by cheer
that's enlivening the whole street.

It's getting on for closing time.
"One more?" bartender touts.
Rational thoughts are rationed
like excuses to a spouse.

Earl Grey's the world's best IPA hands down,
if there were ever doubt.
If this stuff came out of my taps at home
I'd never leave the house.

We're embracing not escaping,
we're building community.
Loneliness's hole is gaping
and we're filling it with glee.

Counsel, comfort and joy
are provided abundantly.
On this whole entire planet,
there's nowhere else I'd rather be.

Quizmastering at The Marble Arch.

1991, it had been in use since.
For years, it fermented creative juices.
Hosted many a great band and singer's debut sets,
but in 2014, it became a nuisance.

The promoters, bartenders, managers and bands,
the door staff, the chefs, the techies and stage hands,
the roadies, the DJs, their tribes and their clans
were told desist or pay a fine of twenty grand.

Complaints from new neighbours on noise did give rise to
authorities snooping, its doors they did pry through
with disapproving made-up minds; it's suffice to
say landlords and spivs were willingly unwise to

the things that hold a community together,
the birthplace of many of music's bellwether,
a home for the tryers, doers and trendsetters.
They thought they'd disperse if they ramped up the pressure.

"You cloister these streets with your music and art.
You loiter entitled, like you've done from the start.
You exploiters of curious, creative hearts.
We're trying to renovate, you're not playing your part!

For a view from the windows of luxury flats,
your creative café seems a bit mismatch.
Close down with congruence or your space we'll snatch.
Stop your music and art and please clean up your act."

If affluence lands and decides to make perch,
should music and art be left out in the lurch?
Should the young minds it nurtures abandon their church?
And their £1.3 billion contribution face purge?

The bigwigs they ceased with their importunity.
The café's still hosting the good and the gritty.
But as they gentrify, we must stand with temerity.
Don't let music and art be forced out of our city.

The Student Maintenance Grant made a paltry sum to 'Pass Go' with in 2011. It has since been changed to a loan, which similarly doesn't stretch far.

Our Guy had been pretty good at maintaining work alongside his studies up to that point, but by the October of that academic year was becoming dejected by the fruitlessness of his distribution of dozens of CVs to bars and restaurants.

His twenty-year-old hedonistic endeavours were never going to be conducive to his shoestring budget stretching to the end of term, so the sense of urgency to find somewhere to pay him £5 an hour to pull pints or serve plates was on a crescendo of serious worry.

One morning, he responded to a vacancy listing on Gumtree. The advert was brief and vague, giving no details of a location, simply listing 'Hospitality Work' as something for which there was a vacancy and informing applicants to send a CV along with a profile picture to an email address.

Later that afternoon, Our Guy received a phone call from The Recruiter regarding his response to the advert listed. The Recruiter was pleasant and complimentary, but concise and matter of fact in his tone. Our Guy eagerly waited for pauses in The Recruiter's spiel to shoehorn in soundbites of his immaculate eligibility to be a bar tender, or waiter, or whatever it was he was recruiting for.

Then, suddenly, The Recruiter dropped a succulent worm of bait into the conversation.

"It's £100 an hour."

Our Guy tried to stifle the awestruck astonishment in his tone as he queried for further detail.

He was biting The Recruiter's hand off through the phone.

"Well, it's not your usual hospitality work, you see," he disclosed. "You would be working on a one-to-one basis with our clients, most of whom are busy businesswomen of middle-age, who are happy to pay for company with which to unwind. Most sessions are around three hours long and you pay a 30% cut of your take back to us."

What did The Recruiter mean?

A private bar tender for one woman? Surely even the super-rich weren't as indolent as to have other people make their drinks at home.

Our Guy's heart began to beat faster, as the exact parameters of what he was getting himself into started to flash in his mind.

"It's usually at this part of the conversation that people change their mind," The Recruiter admitted with jovial candour, "but yes, it's escort work. And whilst I know it's not for everybody, it can be a really good earner."

At the time, Our Guy's romantic pursuits were about as fruitful as his search for work – amplifying his Smiths-sound-tracked post-adolescent loneliness.

Could this be a job opportunity *and a sex opportunity*?

His lustful opportunism and cash-strapped desperation swelled at the potential that lay before him.

The Recruiter politely conceded that if Our Guy hadn't done this kind of work before, then it would take some consideration. However, if he did want to proceed with it, to call The Recruiter back before the end of the week with his decision.

Could he do it?

The ethics of the potential undertaking weren't something that sat comfortably. After the phone call with The Recruiter ended, Our Guy found himself in an increasingly dizzying state of anxiety.

He had a week to fashion a decision out of the trepidation, curiosity and excitement that engulfed him.

Then, at about 3 p.m., his phone went off again.

It was The Recruiter.

He told him that he had an update.

He explained to Our Guy with business-like succinctness that the usual means of advertising and getting the attention of potential clients wasn't something that was viable for his business, given the nature of said business. It was an escort business after all.

He told him that new employees made a one-off contribution of £100 towards the costs incurred in the promotion of them to potential new clients – like an agency fee.

He also told him that he was calling back so soon because he had actually run his profile picture through the business's channels of advertising as a bit of a test and it had already attracted interest, even as far as a regular client asking if she could be seen by Our Guy tonight.

Tonight!

The Recruiter's tone softened as he explained to Our Guy that he wouldn't have usually done that and that Our Guy shouldn't feel pressured to take up the offer and didn't owe him anything for promoting his picture if he decided not to.

"Have a think."

He then gave details of the fifty-something, American business-woman who would be staying in the Hilton on Deansgate that night and wanting to pay for four hours of his company.

He reaffirmed that Our Guy shouldn't feel pressured to, but if he wanted to take up the offer he should send him the £100 contribution by 4 p.m. and he would then give him more detailed instructions on where to meet this woman who would be paying for his company.

Our Guy checked his bank balance and found that he had just shy of £200 remaining. That £100 would halve his already hopelessly inadequate budget for the remainder of the term. However, £280 would be made back by providing his… "Company" (?!!).

Nervousness turned to anxiety, turned to lusty excitement, cycling over and over.

After much hesitation, Our Guy called The Recruiter back and told him that he would like to go ahead with it.

The Recruiter gave Our Guy his bank details, asked him to send £100 there and then and said that he'd call him back afterwards and email over a contract.

Our Guy keyed in numbers on the card reader corresponding to the code on his online banking home page, double-checked The Recruiter's bank details and with trepidation clicked 'Send'.

The money was gone.

Awaiting The Recruiter's phone call, Our Guy chain-smoked and did press ups to psyche himself up.

Half an hour passed and Our Guy started to hanker for clarity on the next steps for his new opportunity – a stone to kill the birds of both his aching loneliness and sexual frustration and his grim financial prognosis for the remainder of the term.

Realising nearly an hour had passed since Our Guy had sent The Recruiter the money, he set a time at which to call him back to check in on what the next steps were.

The wait certainly wasn't helping the nervousness.

The time that Our Guy had mentally set arrived and he went through his recent calls and pressed green on The Recruiter's phone number.

The dissonant three-note melody that proceeded the message of *The number you have dialled has not been recognised* sent a shiver up Our Guy's spine.

How could the number not be recognised?

He'd already made three calls to The Recruiter.

He tried again, then again, then again.

It then hit Our Guy like a deconstructed brick shit-house falling from the sky.

There was no agency.

Our Guy had been scammed out of £100 in attempting to take up an opportunity to become an escort.

What if his friends found out?!

He realised after a few calls to a fraud hotline that there was basically no prospect of him regaining his £100.

Knowing that his twenty-first birthday party was the following week and that the compounded financial hardship combined with the tragic hilarity of the incident weren't something that he could keep secret, Our Guy confided the story with about a dozen of his friends. It predictably resulted in a deluge of pictures of Ford Escorts being posted down his Facebook timeline.

Sex workers, a majority of whom are women, face a stigmatised, un-unionised and often dangerous plight. Their work is work and they should be supported, listened to and protected from the dangers they face.

I think it's safe to say that Our Guy got off lucky with his hapless £100 loss.

III : How I made my millions

I write this from the kitchen of the house that my best friend Paul has bought. He has a proper, well-paid job and is renting a room to me for £250 a month less than I was paying previously.

My wonderful girlfriend, Jenny, lent me a bit of money this month and – amongst other things – has patiently and attentively listened to drafts of different pieces from this book.

I have been given the opportunity to write this book by Flapjack Press and inspired by poets who have become some of my closest friends; friends who have afforded me countless opportunities to perform and helped me to equip myself to set this poetry lark up as a proper career.

I have been mentored in my writing and performing by many such poets and prominently by Dominic Berry, who has challenged and encouraged me with genuinely constructive and stimulating feedback. He is a great mentor and even better friend.

I have been in receipt of a gargantuan amount of generosity from such a number of different people for all of my thirty years and I am so full of gratitude. It pains me that it would be beyond what is practical in the introduction of a poetry book to go into much more depth on that point.

The person whose generosity I have had bestowed upon me most – and the person whose support and encouragement has been most enduring – is my Mum, Lin.

I am from a single parent family, having been estranged from my Dad from when I was fourteen. Whilst he made a marked impression on my life and early upbringing, it is an impression that is as fraught with traumas as it is fond memories or inspiration – so I'll leave it at that, on him.

My Mum had to retire early following a mental health crisis and brought me and my little sister, Heather, up in the leafy middle-class Cheshire town of Congleton.

We were immensely fortuitous to have grown up in the New Labour era, when the relative compassion of the welfare state allowed us free school meals, support workers to help in tasks my Mum struggled with, and allowed us to stay in the nice three-bedroom semi-detached house that my Mum had bought with my Dad when they were together.

My Mum was ceaselessly supportive – even if her support wasn't something I recognised at the time.

As most creatively inclined people do, I have been often in need of being knocked down a peg or two. My Mum's wit provided this in the most poetic of ways.

I remember, after moving home for a twelve-month spell when I'd got myself into credit card and pay day loan debt in Manchester, I went out on a date in my home town.

The date didn't go very well. When I arrived home, I was greeted by my Mum inquisitively enquiring:

"Well, how did it go?"

"It didn't go all that well, Mum," I responded.

"Oh, Rob. A good shag would cheer you up as well, wouldn't it?!"

My Mum had found solace, hope and recovery from the turmoil of ill mental health in the Christian faith. Whilst she never cast dogmatic moral judgements on my behaviour as an adolescent, the implied presence of religious dogma made for a funny juxtaposition with what I was getting up to in Manchester.

Not long after graduating, I had some work as an extra in the Russell T. Davies, Channel 4, LGBTQ+ comedy drama, *Cucumber*.

When the first episode aired, I had a call from my Mum:

"Have you watched it?" she asked.

"I haven't gotten around to it yet Mum, I'm going to watch it on 4OD," I replied.

"Well!" she exclaimed, in a startled tone. "I just wish you'd told *me the show was all about willies before I got all of my friends at church to watch it!"*

My Mum had been a teacher before she retired and was brilliant at instilling in me a yearning for learning. Whilst struggling with reading (which I later discovered dyslexia and dyspraxia were factors in), I was adamantly keen to express myself orally (not in *that* way).

I was in a weird purgatory of social status at school, where I'd be picked on for being well-spoken and eloquent (my nickname when I visit my home town is still Well-Spoken Rob), but also picked on by the posh kids for getting free school meal tokens.

In nurturing my development and pursuits as a musician, my Mum instilled in me a strong will to have creative outlets with which to express myself, which ultimately mutated to the contents of this book.

Manchester was the Muse for – and setting of – the first steps on my poetry journey. It is host to the most amazing people, as I hope I have conveyed in the previous chapter.

In this concluding chapter, I pay tribute to those with whom I've grown up and spent the most time with; to their quirks and intricacies. They continue to inspire me every day (even if it is just to wise-crack about).

My wealth *is* the people around me.

Man o' the House

For Linda, my marvellous Mum.

Man o' the house now!
House-man.
Houseman.
That's what they told her infant son.
Before you've learned to walk
you must get on your feet and run.
You're only four years clear of learning
to wipe your own bum.
It appears you're the right gender
and every house must have one.

Y'know, like a drawer stuffed with plastic bags...

A man o' the house screws lids off jars
with his Y chromosome.
Every house needs a man, y'see,
manliness you should hone.
Pull your socks up son,
moss can't grow on a rolling stone.
As if a seven-year-old's strength
could be a pillar to her home.

You might think *ah, man o' the house,*
well, this could make the best of me.
Well, hold your horses son,
this house is in negative equity.
Now get on manning-up young boy,
you're hardly houseman pedigree.
Your Mum's sick in the head, y'see,
better hope it's not hereditary.

She's not in great nick they told him.
Step up! they implored.
She's had to spend some time
inside a psychiatric ward.
Her words illuminated by gaslight
to the two she adored.
Despite her devotion persisting
since they cut umbilical cords.

She'd retired from teaching early,
but never ceased to be a teacher.
She reached all learning outcomes
despite veering from procedure.
Things tidy not, but defying odds
brought two kids through the ether.
The thankless tasks those two kids left…
No grim task was beneath her.

Changing the oil in a car,
re-felting a leaky roof,
safely chopping down a tree,
she taught him in his youth.
She'd watch with discernment
when he got too big for his boots.
And when necessary,
she would knock him down a peg or two.

Like
when, at twenty-four, he boastfully showed a picture of his new fling
on his phone, she responded, "Gosh, Rob, has she got a guide dog?"

Or when, at fourteen, she picked him up after he'd passed out and
projectile vomited on his paper round following an evening of underage
drinking and said nothing, leaving it to him to admit he was reaping
what he had sowed.

Facebook market, charity shop finds
keep her heart a-boon.
Numerous white elephants
fill up all her rooms.
(These white elephants though,
they're gifts to friends, not useless heirlooms.)
Thirty years ago, she played guitar
to him inside her womb.

But him;
his masculine-a-quest sequestered not,
he yearned to manly summit.
He found a manly task to do,
but she'd already done it.
He read about how men won bread,
but she'd already won it!
The web that kept them safe,
it was his Mother who had spun it.

Man o' the house, eh?

This supposed role's superfluous,
there was no needed plan.
Against the toils that followed,
it was *her* who had the upper hand.
The ignorant around them,
they just didn't understand.
For with his Mother holding fort,
their house didn't need a Man.

Bedsheets

A triolet.

I'm jealous of your bedsheets
        clinging to you.
    I'd kill to be as close to you as them,
        each morning savour.
     Like Jack and Kate on morning's bow,
          this bedsheet sea we move through.

I'm jealous of your bedsheets
        clinging to you.
    The scent of you
        leaves anxieties subdued.
    The taste of you,
        I'd make into an ice cream flavour.

I'm jealous of your bedsheets
        clinging to you.
    I'd kill to be as close to you as them,
        each morning savour.

Between Them

A univocalism in 'E'.

She's here.
Yes.
Her presence,
he begs.
Her effervescent sweetness,
he's beset.
Her cheeks red,
he expects.

Debted, he jests best,
vested, presently ... sex.
They decree between them,
lest we stress,
lest we regret.
He behests
her French kecks gently shed.
He expresses
let's be messes.
Better yet,
drench bedsheets,
yell yesses,
yell yesses.
Yes.

He sees her chest;
bejewelled refreshments,
her perfect flesh.
She seeps wet, tempts.
She then de-dresses.

He de-dresses.
He redresses empress's deserved glee.
Vehemently, relentlessly they vent.

Between them,
synergy.
Between them,
best yet.
Between them,
perfect.
Between them,
yes.

Stunners

For Paul, another bloody triolet.

With sardonic solidarity
   your mocking soothes my stress.
  You tell me you don't care,
    but I am not that gullible.
  I'm relieved of my need
    to get all my worries off my chest.

With sardonic solidarity
   your mocking soothes my stress.
  Sometimes I need to be reminded
   the best remedy is jest.
  My date went well, you say:
    "She'll find out you're unlovable."

With sardonic solidarity
   your mocking soothes my stress.
  You tell me you don't care,
    but I am not that gullible.

Feeling This

For Ollie.

The rays of the sun didn't travel
149,600,000 kilometres
undisturbed,
only to be obstructed by my body,
stationary.

Patiently, the skins on each head
anticipate my blistered,
calloused five digits, gripping
Vic Firths [7], inducing fidgets and twerks
and head-bopping unanimity.

Synergy
is what the four of us are feeling
and to apathy and depression we bring
healing.

And in empathy,
camaraderie and rhythm
we are dealing
and our mission this evening
is to raise the fucking ceiling,

'cause if you ain't down to groove,
or simply nod in solidarity,
we can't meet in the middle,
'cause I'll incite
compulsive muscle spasms
with each sleek paradiddle.

And my comrade
with a bass guitar
will fill your belly
with gut-wrenching frequencies,
shrill saxophone squeals
send your train of thought
on a collision course
with no regard for decency.

Riffs and licks
from strings and a pick
send serotonin
washing each brain cell
in love and funk,
equally.

Y'know why they call it funk?
Because it sounds like fuck.

And you know that with
that kinky combination of
kick, hat, snare,

even the most prudish of people
lose their inhibitions and succumb
to the urge to fuck the air.

Tonight,
we don't care.

We're naked in the intricate
abandonment of ego.
We're lustful for melody
and fuelled with a musical libido.

Synapses fire,
we require
your complete
participation.

This is a musical orgy,
not musical masturbation.
I see, above the parapet
of my Zildjian custom cymbals,
hips swivelling and booties shakin'
and feet movin' in a nimble

celebration of the beauty
and fragility of existence.

One more pass of through the chorus
brings us all crashing to the cadence.
The conclusion brings us all to sweaty,
post-orgasmic bliss.

Nods and winks
and laughs and cheers
confirm we were all
feeling this.

---

[7] Vic Firth was, for the uninitiated, an American percussionist and principal timpanist with the Boston Symphony Orchestra for nearly fifty years. He founded Vic Firth Co., manufacturers of percussion mallets, batons and beaters.[8]

[8] AKA, again for the uninitiated, drumsticks.

Thought Glans

In Memoriam, Dan Price [1992-2017].

Abundantly, the fun it seems is overflowing.
Like bumblebees collecting pollen, growing.
Humbly you question all I'm germinating, sowing.
It's 2010, I'm twenty and you're eighteen
and upon me sweet harmonies, sagacious lyrics,
sincere friendship you're bestowing.
> *And the Irwell keeps a-flowin',*
> *but now there's no way of knowin'.*

A verbal salad conjures theories we were supposedly learning,
dressed with all the adult responsibility we've been adjourning.
In synergy and major keys we find our common yearning
and your blind but perfect intuition for song has started burning.
> *And the Irwell keeps a-flowin',*
> *but now there's no way of knowin'.*

You confess in your exam you had just copied all the answers.
Hours earlier we're graceless in drug-addled dances,
but fuck, nobody more deserved just a few more chances.
Like a psychic night cancelled due to unforeseen circumstances.
> *And the Irwell keeps a-flowin',*
> *but now there's no way of knowin'.*

One example of your daft antics is etched into my memory
and never will it cease to make my sides split so easily.

> I'm cycling up Princess Road en route to
> practise drums to your new songs.
> I pull over to tend to the vibrations
> coming from my phone.

It's you. *"What's up mate?!"* I say.
Your sheepish, conciliatory tone
warms my bones on the cold winter's day.

"I'm so sorry Rob, I..."
"Everything alright mate?!"
Had something terrible happened?

"I'm gonna have to cancel the practice, I'm so sorry, butt.
See, last night the girls in halls were all getting on it,
so I got two bottles of White Ace and joined in.
Anyway boyo, short story long,
I can't remember a fucking thing,
but I woke up this morning and it turns out
I'd done a shit in the sink.
Please don't be mad."

Creasing up, I straighten my bike
and respond reassuringly:
"I could never be mad with you mate.
Shit happens."

I ripped a roach from your business card
and rolled it in a spliff.
A scatty incoherent homage
to your memory is this...

A companion and a support that I felt the need to hide.
He'd sit in silence listening as I'd confess and confide.
Even when told to let him go, I kept him by my side –
to deny him completely, it seemed cruel and it seemed snide.

Content to hang around
and just procrastinate alone,
he spares judgements or assumptions,
few know me better than he knows me.

For years and years I've been soothed
and assured by the love he shows me.
I suppose it makes up for the years
of unpaid rent that he still owes me.

I'm greeted every morning by his still and tranquil stare.
Whilst I'm out earning a living, he's lounging without a care.
If I bring a date back to my flat for sex, you bet, he's there.
I am a thirty-year-old man, who still has his childhood bear.

Moonstruck (Part I)

A flamenca for Jenny.

I gracelessly keep time,
loosing count of 4/4.
You gracefully join
and dance, enchanting me.
My timing is restored.

Your feet choreographed,
mine falling off the floor.
Intrigue waxing large
while apprehension wanes.
I'm moonstruck and in awe.

Moonstruck (Part II)

For Jenny.

You left your toothbrush in my bathroom, leaving one morning.
It made friends with mine and got comfortable over the sink.
It was a memento of your presence, my bathroom adorning.
It watched me showering nude, *the pervert*, flushing my face pink.

The night before we'd met for the first time, under moonlight.
The moon waxing gibbous, the streets – our parabolic paths.
Me, eclipsed with intrigue and attraction as our paths collide.
Serendipitous silliness, my hopeless humour made you laugh.

Records spinning, dancing in the kitchen, each flirty footstep.
The world, distant downstairs, us naked, not giving a shit.
I told you you're beautiful, you smugly responded with *"Yep"*.
Our moves synchronised and we fell comfortably in orbit.

Our moves keep time to a slow meter that's cool in each sway.
Like your image evoked from the sight of a record sleeve.
Moves like me thinking your toothbrush in my bathroom should stay.
Moves like your underwear left on my bed when you leave.

Us sauntering streets, passers-by sickened and I don't mind.
I want more permanence of your presence like the stars above me.
Laughing each other's pain away, our solace aligned.
Like galaxies, you seem so achingly rare and lovely.

With you, I am sure. I'm Moonstruck and in awe,
I've found someone who I want to quit smoking for;
a future with memories – keep making more.
The whole of you, I don't want to cease to explore.

We may wax and wane, injuries we'll sustain,
from some fights we'll abstain and life will inflict pain.
But in orbit we'll wax and in orbit we'll wane.
And in orbit together for long we'll remain.

You left your toothbrush in my bathroom again this morning.
I noticed again and I thought of our orbit for hours.
How a permanence of our waxing and our waning is dawning.
I'm hoping that one day we'll have a bathroom we call ours.

Dumbstruck by Fucks

A univocalic haiku in 'U'. [9]

Cry my guts up dry.
My luck stumps up – lustful crush.
Dumbstruck by fuck thrusts.

---

[9] This univocalism in 'U' replaces one originally written about a buttplug. No matter how hard I tried, it just wouldn't fit.

Be My Quentin Blake

A sonnet for Sonny.

More than his work in the *Washington Post*.
More than the Google doodle he designed.
Achievements that on his behalf I boast.
A man with whom my ups and downs entwined.

A teenage rhythm section that evolved.
Scenes moved from conspiracy conjecture.
Scenes moved from debauched gigs as we got old.
Now we're high off shades and chunky textures.

Art in finding beauty in the mistakes.
Art in joy born from dark introspection.
I wonder if he'd be my Quentin Blake
and illustrate my debut collection.

I remind myself in depressive states
there's art in having maintained such good mates.

The Bucket

Bite off more than you can chew
and then just fucking chew it.
Drop your paddle deep in Shit Creek
and then just row right through it.
Failure's your foul-weather friend,
don't attempt to undo it.
So, kiss its face and embrace gladly
that this time, you blew it.

There's a bucket in your room,
it's filled with shit, it stinks of shame.
The urge to kick the bucket takes up
all of your strength to refrain.
You can stew amongst this stench
or you can pour it down the drain.
Just know that each storm, even this storm,
will run out of rain.

So, wait. Just wait.
Let it throb while you abate.
Know that you are just a visitor,
you are not an inmate.
Know that this is just their gambit,
know that this is not checkmate.
You know you can't have the last laugh
whilst your face is filled with hate.

That bucket, it is gone now.
You stood strong for no evasion.
Last night your entourage of one
summoned the strength of many nations.

You saw how little is conceived
through bitter tears and masturbation.
Your soul's crannies and its nooks
sustained a fierce fumigation.

Now
allow morning's shards of light
to stab you right square in the chest.
Measure this day not in cigarettes,
but in satisfied breaths.
Measure this day not in dividends,
but in yourself invest.
Then at dawn, track down your lover
and lay your head upon their breast.

Tonight, you'll bask in the glorious gloom
of your room, all moonlit.
Dispose of the gun, self-reconstruct,
disassemble your doom-kit.
Drop your paddle deep in Shit Creek
and then just row right through it.
Bite off more than you can chew
and then just fucking chew it.

Finding the comedy in tragedy capitalises on the tragedy in a way completely distinct from the way Our Guy did, once in 2011 and once in 2016.

He had never had any kind of affinity for gambling; partly because of his awareness of his already well-developed skills in frittering away money and partly because one of the first jobs he had as a student was as a cocktail waiter in a casino, where he witnessed the despairing dejection of people's failed flutters.

He similarly didn't have much of an affinity for football, but had been taken to see Stoke City play on a regular basis by his Dad, as a young child.

When Stoke reached the FA Cup final, against all odds in 2011, he was charmed by the underdog spirit and community gathering that it bought about.

Our Guy joined a bunch of mates to watch Stoke City v Manchester City at his local and to show support for the team he had been taken to see. His football fan imposter syndrome was quelled by the spirit of celebration that their progression to the final had brought about.

He decided that a little flutter with the affordable and relatively inconsequential sum of £10 wouldn't do any harm. So, he logged on to a betting website and spread this £10 across a score card that held a variety of goal scoring outcomes.

He had considered betting on Stoke to be victorious, but also knew – even with his very limited knowledge of football – that the odds weren't in their favour. He wanted Stoke to win, so why not set himself up a potential consolation prize for if that didn't occur?

Kick-off arrived, and a standard ninety minutes of shouting, suspense and waiting around aimlessly for people to take free kicks ensued.

Stoke lost 1-0 and the inevitable dejection was levelled out amongst the rowdy pub of Stoke fans with a sense of pride that they'd made it so far.

Our Guy logged back on to the betting website to check the outcome of his bet and found that he had, without realising it, bet the correct final score, the correct goal scorer and the correct half of the goal. This trifecta resulted in his paltry £10 being turned into the tidy sum of £140.

He was quids in!

Aware of the pitfalls of gambling, Our Guy quit whilst he was ahead and never felt tempted to indulge in such an act again.

Then, in 2016, Donald Trump stood for the Presidency of the United States. How desperately undesirable an outcome his success would be to a bleeding-heart socialist like Our Guy is a point that needs no labouring. When the *Access Hollywood* tapes of Donald Trump bragging about sexual assault emerged, Our Guy figured his odds would have significantly dropped, so as with Stoke losing the FA Cup final, he thought that in the complete worst case scenario of him being successful, he ought to line up himself a small financial consolation prize.

Needless to say, Our Guy has opted to never place a bet again.

Whilst a mere two instances of him winning a financial reward from undesirable outcomes isn't enough to constitute hard evidence, it is still probably best for Our Guy to believe that he has the power to jinx positive outcomes by betting against them.

Let's face it – no amount of money would have been a big enough consolation prize for the victory of Donald Trump.

I came alone to the bar after work, but his gaze caught me.
His Beamer parked obstructing access to the path, all haughty.
His personalised numberplate should read TW4T.
The condescending quips come quick at me, like I've been naughty.

"I'm a self-made millionaire," he proclaims. *"Self-made millionaire!*
Just my own hard graft that got me here, no handouts or welfare."
I humour this chap's hubris and ask if his secret he'd share.
"Private equity, private investments and private healthcare.

No fancy university degree for me," he boasts.
"Got in the money game early and before long I was engrossed.
I had to find my own way; the path was without signposts.
Inheritance? Of course, but compared to what I've now grossed

my merited affluence – it pales – really wasn't much.
My eminence in profit, you could say it was my crutch.
Whilst decadent and elegant, I still have the common touch.
This talk of raising taxes to me just seems double Dutch.

Paid severance to some bolshie ex-worker who rebelled,
just yesterday! My lawyers said that my defence was quelled.
I'm wrong, apparently, because his wages I'd withheld.
I know right?! Forty staff who all work for me, haven't I excelled?

I mean technically they're all self-employed – it's like an outgoings
reduction.
I pay enough out in my taxes to pay scroungers who can't function
and those who've not reached such heights as mine must just lack the
guts and gumption.
A simple lack of hard work seems a reasonable assumption.

I'm a wealth maker! Yeah... wealth-maker, that seems an apt description.
My twelve acres in Provence came with much hard graft and friction.
Sick of hearing about those for whom a lack of wealth's an affliction.
I just can't stop making wealth...
Oh... but it's not like an addiction."

I sit wishing I'd never asked of how he made his millions,
affixed whiffing his putrid breath and obnoxious opinions.
My mind wonders to what really constitutes human brilliance.
Not belligerent bourgie boast, but kindness and resilience.

I think of the teachers who teach this arrogant bastard's kids at school.
I stare at the ground beneath us as he goes on from his bar stool
to avoid being subjected to his barrage of boasts and drool.
Sharp-elbowed pricks like this have flourished under Tory rule.

I think of the nurse whose eyes momentarily slumped in sleep
whilst assessing me at 3 a.m. in A&E last week.
Her – stoic and determined, in a setting cold and bleak.
Her – resolute, in a ward with capacity at peak.

I think of the carers who care for my Nan, day in, day out,
such bearers of hard graft that no-one in their right mind may doubt
their immeasurable value, the nurturing they lay out.
It's all rewarded with a meagre minimum wage pay-out.

The social workers, support workers, counsellors and nurses.
The bar staff, techies, singers and poets, who in joy immerse us.
We contribute in taxes and their efforts reimburse us.
If merit meant anything there'd be millions in their purses.